One Burner Man
© 2025 Barbara Nelson Bennett and Delroy Bennett
All rights reserved.

Published by New Being Books (Lauderhill, Florida)
Cover Art by Gabyriella Foster
ISBN: 979-8-9918479-3-3

Unless otherwise indicated, all Scripture quotations are taken from the New Living Translation (NLT) via the YouVersion Bible App. NLT copyright © 1996, 2004, 2015

This book is written to encourage, uplift, and inspire readers with biblical wisdom and practical life application. It is not intended as a substitute for professional counseling or pastoral guidance.

Printed in the United States of America
First Edition, 2025

To every man ready to choose covenant over culture—
This book is for you.
For the one who dares to burn for one woman,
To love deeply, lead faithfully, and live fully surrendered to God.
May these words strengthen your steps,
And may your life reflect the fire of a true kingdom man—
A **one burner** man.

To the man who showed me it was possible to love one woman

Barbara Nelson Bennett

One Burner Man

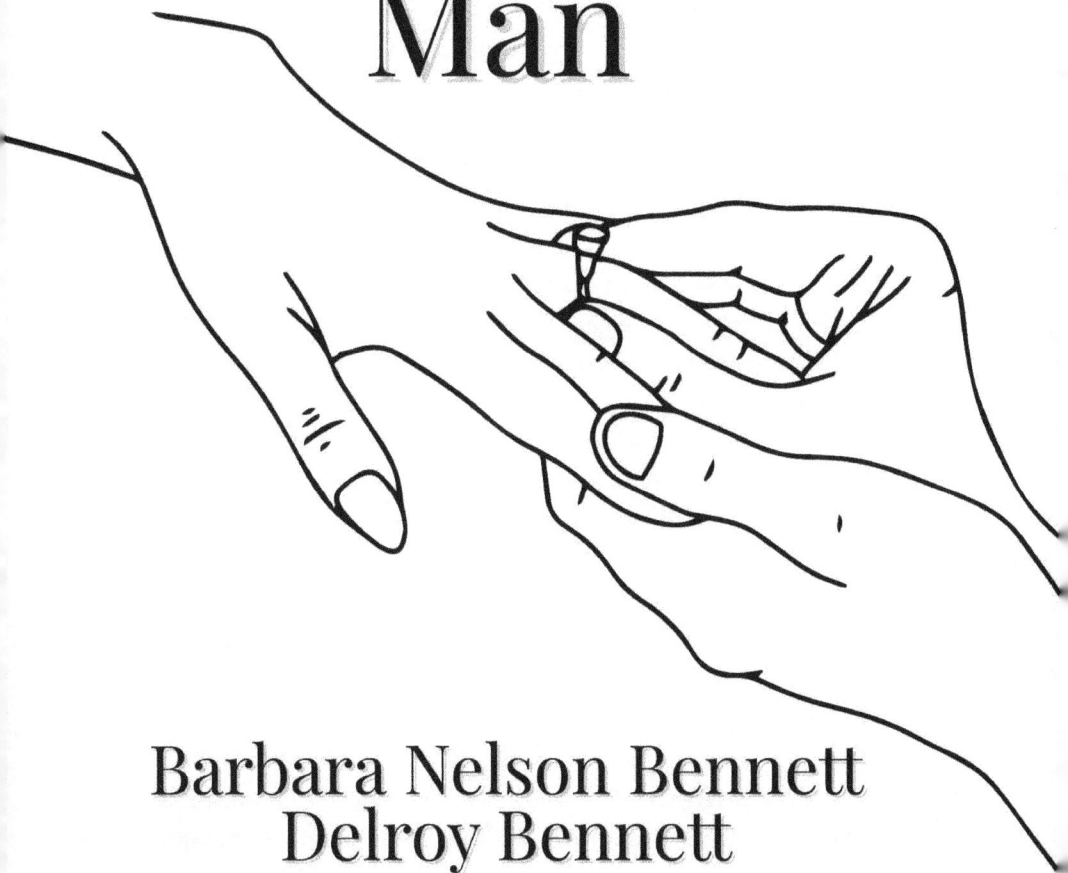

Barbara Nelson Bennett
Delroy Bennett

Author's Note

I met Delroy ten years ago. Our courtship was swift, our commitment immediate. We didn't need time to deliberate—we knew. From the beginning, we set clear boundaries: exclusivity, discretion, and the sanctity of a small, trusted circle. He was shaped by his father's failings, molded by the pain of divided loyalties. Delroy chose differently. He chose loyalty. He chose me. And he never looked back.

He wasn't a man of many friendships. His world revolved around family. He believed in the sanctity of home and the quiet strength of togetherness. For him, life was not about individual pursuits, but shared purpose. He believed that most things were better done side by side.

In an age that celebrates multitasking and the relentless chase for more—more success, more status, more everything—Delroy moves against the current. He is, unapologetically, a "one-burner man." While others divide their focus among careers, accolades, and social ambition, Delroy directs his flame wholly toward one unwavering priority: family.

His life is a testament to the quiet power of focus. He believes that to do everything is often to do nothing well. And so, he has made a conscious choice—to pour his time, his energy, and his heart into the people he loves. That's where his flame burns brightest. Whether it's cheering from the front row at school plays, mending what's broken around the house, or sitting with me in the stillness of the evening, his presence is both steady and profound. In these everyday moments, he reveals a truth: consistency is a powerful form of love. There is a grounded dignity in the way Delroy moves through life. He doesn't rely on grand gestures or declarations. His love simmers—not flashy, not loud, but enduring. He shows up. Fully. He listens with intention, supports without condition, and leads not with words, but with action.

To some, the one-burner lifestyle may seem limiting. But for me, it has been profoundly liberating. Delroy has taught me that when you know what matters most, the rest has a way of aligning. His focus on family isn't a lack of ambition—it's the highest form of it. He's invested in something deeper than accolades: a home rooted in love, shaped by stability, and full of meaning.

Delroy may not chase everything. But what he does pursue—us—he protects, nurtures, and holds with both hands. For that, he's more than a husband. He is the anchor of our lives.

Ten years with one person will test everything—your patience, your trust, your love, even your sense of humor. But through it all, Delroy has remained constant—not just my partner, but my confidant and greatest champion. Life's storms have come and gone, but never once did I doubt where his heart was. His loyalty was never performative. It was found in the smallest details: remembering how I take my tea, checking in just because, being home when it matters most.

Delroy might be a one-burner man—but that doesn't make him simple. It makes him rare.

Barbara Nelson Bennett

Table of Contents

Preface

We are living in a time where commitment has lost its value. A time where faithfulness is mocked, and marriage is treated like an outdated institution rather than the sacred covenant God designed it to be. The world tells men they can have as many women as they want, that settling down is a limitation, that loyalty is optional. Infidelity is normalized, broken homes are expected, and leadership in the home has been replaced by passivity or domination—neither of which reflect God's design.

But we refuse to accept this.

Marriage was never meant to be a temporary arrangement or a convenience based on feelings. It was created by God as a reflection of His love, His order, and His faithfulness. A One Burner Man is a man who understands this. He is a man who burns with passion, devotion, and commitment for one woman, and one woman only. He does not entertain distractions. He does not waver. His love is steadfast, fueled not by mere emotion but by conviction, discipline, and the power of God.

Being a One Burner Man is more than just staying faithful—it is about becoming a kingdom husband. A man who leads, not by control, but by example. A man who covers his wife in prayer, protects her with wisdom, and builds his home on the foundation of Christ. A man who understands that true strength is not in how many women he can have, but in how well he can love, serve, and remain devoted to the one God has given him.

This book is a guide for men who want more than what the world offers—men who want to live in purpose, honor, and divine order. Through biblical wisdom, real-life testimonies, and practical application, this book will equip you to become the husband, leader, and protector that God has called you to be.

Each chapter is designed to challenge you, refine you, and elevate you. You will find scriptures to ground you, prayers to strengthen you, and reflections to deepen your understanding of what it means to love one woman like Christ loves the Church.

This is not just a book—it is a call to rise. A call to break generational cycles, to stand as a pillar of strength, and to embrace a love that is sacred, unwavering, and ordained by God.

Are you ready to walk in your calling as a One Burner Man?

CHAPTER ONE
It Starts in the Mind

A man doesn't become a One Burner Man by accident. It's not just about saying, "I'll be faithful." It's a mindset. A decision. A lifestyle.

The world tells men that faithfulness is boring, that commitment is restrictive, that having options is what makes you a man. But let me tell you this—true strength is in discipline, not in indulgence. A man who is led by every desire, every temptation, every passing pleasure is not a strong man. He is a slave to his own flesh. But a One Burner Man? He is a man of focus, conviction, and integrity.

In a world where commitment is seen as limitation and faithfulness as old-fashioned, the idea of a One Burner Man stands as a blazing contradiction. Society tells men to keep their options open, to never settle, to chase pleasure and variety as if love is something to be consumed and discarded like fast food. But a One Burner Man is not swayed by the culture—he is a man who has chosen to burn for one woman, to love one woman, to honor one woman.

A man with one burner doesn't split his fire, doesn't cook on many stoves, doesn't entertain distractions. He tends to one flame, one pot, one meal—because he understands that true intimacy and legacy are built in the consistency of undivided and undiluted love. Imagine a stove with four burners. Some men have all four turned on—one for their wife, one for their side woman, one for secret temptations, and one for anything else that catches their eye. Their fire is scattered, weak, inconsistent. But a One Burner Man? He has one flame, one fire, one focus. His love doesn't flicker between different women—it burns hot, steady, and strong for the one God has given him. A One Burner Man understands that his relationship is a reflection of his walk with God. Just like how Christ is faithful to His Church, a man is called to be faithful to his wife.

Proverbs 5:18
Let your fountain be blessed, and rejoice with the wife of your youth.

The world teaches men to be like wildfire, burning through relationships, never staying, never building, never rooted. But wildfire destroys—it leaves nothing but ashes in its wake. A One Burner Man, however, is like the fire in a lighthouse, steady, unmoved, a guide in the storm. His love is not reckless; it is intentional. He is a man who understands that marriage is not a contract but a covenant, a sacred agreement before God where love is not based on convenience but on commitment. The enemy of our souls has long been on a mission to distort what God designed.

Marriage was God's idea, but society has made it seem unnecessary, like an outdated tradition instead of a divine institution.

The enemy whispers:

- "Why settle down? There are too many options."
- "Marriage will hold you back."
- "You can love her but still entertain others."

But the Bible speaks a different word:

---·---

Proverbs 5:15-16

Drink water from your own cistern, running water from your own well. Should your springs overflow in the streets, your streams of water in the public squares?"

---·---

A One Burner Man guards his well. He does not let his love be poured out recklessly. He knows that what is sacred must be protected. A One Burner Man is not just a faithful man—he is a kingdom husband, a man who leads with wisdom, patience, and love. He is a man after God's own heart, and because of that, he loves his wife not just with words but with action, sacrifice, and unwavering dedication. A house built on sand cannot stand, and in the same way, a relationship built on anything other than God's design will eventually collapse. The world builds on feelings, on fleeting attraction, on temporary excitement, but a One Burner Man builds on truth, integrity, and a covenant mindset. Think about a house built in a hurricane-prone area. If the foundation is weak, the first storm will tear it apart. But when a house is built with reinforced concrete, with deep-rooted pillars, it can withstand the wind, the rain, the shaking. That's the difference between a man who is led by desires versus a man who is led by principles. Before a man ever betrays his wife, before he ever gives in to temptation, before he ever entertains another woman—**he has already lost the battle in his mind.**

The mind is the battlefield where faithfulness is either won or lost. Long before a man steps out, **he has already stepped away in his thoughts.** The first compromise is not the text message, the flirtation, or the secrecy—it's the thought that says:

- "There's nothing wrong with just looking."
- "I'm not doing anything—just having fun."
- "She doesn't understand me like this other woman does."
- "I'm a good man; this one mistake won't change that."

But what starts as a whisper in the mind becomes a fire in the soul. A single unchecked thought is like a match struck in a dry forest—it seems small, but left alone, it will burn everything down. **The Bible warns us:**

Proverbs 23:7
For as he thinketh in his heart, so is he.

A man becomes what he dwells on. If his mind is filled with comparison, lust, fantasy, and selfishness, then his actions will inevitably follow. But a man who has trained his mind to be disciplined, honorable, and focused on truth will walk in faithfulness long before it is tested. **How to Win the Battle in the Mind:**

Take Every Thought Captive

Lust doesn't start as a shout—it starts as a whisper. A thought enters the mind, and if left unchecked, it grows. It becomes a fantasy, a craving, a desire, and eventually an action. A One Burner Man doesn't entertain daydreams of another woman, what-ifs, or curious flirtations. **Instead, he does what the Bible commands:**

------------ · ------------

2 Corinthians 10:5
Take captive every thought to make it obedient to Christ.

------------ · ------------

- When a tempting thought enters, immediately reject it. Say out loud, "That is not who I am."
- Replace it with truth. Think of your wife, your vows, your legacy, and the destruction that comes from unfaithfulness.
- Pray in that moment. Ask God to renew your mind.

Practical Steps: How to Become a One Burner Man

1.Guard Your Eyes, Guard Your Heart
- Set boundaries with social media and

- entertainment. Avoid indulging in content that glorifies infidelity or objectifies women.
- Be mindful of friendships with the opposite sex. Emotional affairs often start with "harmless" conversations.
- Redirect your thoughts. When tempted, remind yourself of your wife's value and the commitment you made before God.

Job 31:1

I made a covenant with my eyes not to look lustfully at a young woman

---

2. Be a Pursuer, Not Just a Provider

- Date her even after marriage. A wife who is cherished doesn't have to wonder if she is enough.
- Speak her love language. Learn what makes her feel loved— whether it's words, gifts, acts of service, time, or physical affection.
- Pray with her. A house built on prayer cannot be easily shaken.

3. Cut Off Any Plan B

- No secret conversations. Delete the number, end the text thread, unfollow if necessary.
- Be transparent. If you wouldn't say or do it in front of your wife, don't entertain it at all.

- Accountability matters. Surround yourself with other men of integrity who will call you higher.

A One Burner Man understands that love is not just a feeling—it is a discipline. Just as a fire needs tending, love needs investment. A man does not wake up one day and magically become faithful—he chooses faithfulness every day. He guards his eyes, his heart, and his mind.

- **He does not entertain flirtation that leads to temptation.**
- **He does not plant seeds of discontent by comparing his wife to another woman.**
- **He does not leave doors open for the enemy to walk in.**

Instead, he cultivates love, he pursues his wife daily, he keeps his fire burning only for her.

Conclusion

A One Burner Man wins the battle in the mind before he ever faces the temptation in the world. The way you think today is shaping the man you will be tomorrow. If your thoughts are undisciplined, if you allow small compromises, if you let seeds of dissatisfaction grow—then the harvest will be unfaithfulness, regret, and broken trust. But if you guard your mind like a fortress, if you train yourself in discipline, if you fill your heart with love, integrity, and commitment—then you will be a man who can look back and say: "I have burned for one woman, and one woman only.

My fire has never wavered."

Prayer

Father, You are the ultimate example of covenant love. You have never left us, never forsaken us, never given Your love in pieces. Teach me to love as You love. Help me to be a man of integrity, a man of one fire, one devotion, one love. You created my mind to reflect Your truth, not the world's deception. Help me to guard my thoughts, to reject what is not of You, and to dwell on what is good, pure, and honorable. Strengthen me to be faithful in my heart before I am ever tested in my actions. Let my love be undivided, my devotion be pure, and my mind be focused on my wife alone. **In Jesus' name, Amen**

REFLECTION

What thoughts have I entertained that do not align with faithfulness?

_____

_____

_____

_____

_____

_____

_____

_____

_____

_____

_____

_____

_____

_____

_____

_____

_____

_____

_____

_____

_____

_____

REFLECTION

Do I allow small compromises in my mind that could grow
into something bigger?

_____

_____

_____

_____

_____

_____

_____

_____

_____

_____

_____

_____

_____

_____

_____

_____

_____

_____

_____

_____

REFLECTION

How can I guard my eyes, my heart, and my thoughts
more intentionally?

_____

_____

_____

_____

_____

_____

_____

_____

_____

_____

_____

_____

_____

_____

_____

_____

_____

_____

_____

_____

REFLECTION

What steps can I take today to be a man who wins in the
mind before the battle even begins?

_____

_____

_____

_____

_____

_____

_____

_____

_____

_____

_____

_____

_____

_____

_____

_____

_____

_____

CHAPTER TWO

Laying the Foundation
Commitment as a Covenant

Commitment is more than a promise; it is a covenant. A covenant is not just words spoken in a moment of passion or obligation—it is a sacred agreement, a bond that is sealed before God. In today's world, commitment is treated like a contract—something that can be amended, broken, or voided when it no longer serves one's personal desires. But a true man of integrity, a One Burner Man, understands that marriage is not a mere agreement between two people. It is a divine assignment.

The Difference Between a Contract and a Covenant

A contract is based on conditions—"I will do my part as long as you do yours." But a covenant is built on faithfulness, not conditions. It says, "Even when things are hard, even when I don't feel like it, even when challenges arise—I will remain committed." His faithfulness is not just a personal decision—it is a covenant made before God. But what does that really mean? What is the difference between a contract and a covenant? Why does it matter? A contract is built on human terms. A covenant is built on divine principles.

A contract says:

- *"I will do my part as long as you do yours."*
- *"If you stop meeting my needs, I have the right to walk away."*
- *"If circumstances change, this agreement can be renegotiated."*

But a covenant says:

- *"I am committed to you, not just when it's easy, but even when it's hard."*
- *"I will love you, not because of what you give me, but because of who I have chosen you to be."*
- *"This is not about convenience—it's about a calling."*

Contracts are based on mutual benefit. The moment one party fails to meet expectations, the contract can be broken. This is why modern relationships often fail—many men enter marriage with a contract mindset, thinking, "As long as she makes me happy, as long as she meets my needs, I will stay." But what happens when life gets hard? When external pressures come? When emotions fade? A contract-based relationship cannot withstand pressure because it is built on conditions instead of commitment. A covenant is not an agreement—it is a spiritual binding. It is the same type of commitment God makes with His people.

Malachi 2:14
The Lord has been witness between you and the wife of your youth, to whom you have been faithless, though she is your companion and your wife by covenant

God does not see marriage as a piece of paper. He sees it as a sacred bond that reflects His own love for His people. The One Burner Man understands this. He does not see marriage as a disposable agreement but as a lifelong commitment to lead, love, and serve. The Bible gives us a perfect example of covenant love through Christ. The relationship between Christ and the Church is described as a marriage, where Christ is the bridegroom, and we, His people, are the bride.

What kind of love does Christ show us?

- ·He loves us unconditionally – even when we fail, even when we fall short.
- ·He sacrifices for us – He gave His very life for His bride.
- ·He remains faithful – even when we are unfaithful.

This is the standard of covenant love. The One Burner Man is called to love his wife the same way.

——— · ———

Ephesians 5:25

Husbands, love your wives, just as Christ loved the church and gave himself up for her

——— · ———

This means that a true man does not just stay faithful in body, but in heart, mind, and actions. He does not just "stick around" out of obligation—he pours himself out in love, even when it costs him something.

Think about the difference between renting a house and owning one. When you rent, you might take care of the property, but at the end of the day, it doesn't really belong to you. If something breaks, it's not necessarily your responsibility to fix it. If you decide you no longer like the place, you simply pack up and leave. But when you own a home, your mindset is different. You invest in it. You protect it. When problems arise, you fix them because you understand that what you build today will impact the years to come. This is the difference between a contractual marriage and a covenantal one.

- A contract-based marriage is like renting. If things get hard, you consider walking away.
- A covenant-based marriage is like owning. You are invested for life, so you do the work to maintain, restore, and build something lasting.

God calls men to own their marriages, not rent them for convenience.

Love is not just an emotion; it is a decision. Too many men fall into the trap of thinking that commitment should be easy, that as long as love is present, faithfulness will follow effortlessly. But emotions are like the tide—always moving, always changing. A real man does not build his marriage on waves that come and go. He builds it on the rock of conviction, intention, and action. A man who only shows up for his marriage when he feels like it is like a farmer who plants a crop but only waters it when he's in the mood. What happens? The soil dries up. The harvest never comes. Then, when he sees no fruit, he blames the land, when in reality, he never nurtured it properly. Marriage requires daily tending. You don't just commit on your wedding day and coast for the rest of your life. You wake up every morning and choose your wife again. **You choose to:**

- ·Speak life over her when she's weary.
- ·Cover her in prayer when she's anxious.
- ·Protect her heart from anything that might shake her confidence in your love.

Commitment means staying planted even when the season is dry, even when storms come, even when other pastures look greener. Because the truth is—the grass isn't greener on the other side. The grass is greener where you water it. Every man wants to believe he is committed until commitment is tested. It's easy to stand at the altar, look a woman in the eye, and promise "for better or worse." But what happens when the "worse" comes? When life gets heavy, when stress builds, when arguments arise—do you run, or do you dig deeper?

Your commitment to one another, your marriage, it will be tested. It will be tested with fire. Do you know the process a sword has to go through to be made? Metal is heated then beaten and hammered, and finally goes through the fire again. But if the sword does not go through this process, it remains weak and useless. So you see, fire can be deadly. Fire can destroy. But fire, and trials they are the great refiners. When your marriage is tested, when commitment is tested, you become better as a couple and better individually.

Practical Steps, How to Shift from a Contract to a Covenant Mindset:

1. **Decide that Divorce is Not an Option** – When you remove exit doors, you are forced to work through issues instead of running from them. A covenant-minded man fights for his marriage, not against it.

2. **Change How You See Your Role** – You are not just a partner in a relationship; you are a spiritual leader in a covenant. Lead with integrity. Serve with love.

3. **Love as a Choice, Not Just a Feeling** – Feelings fade, but commitment lasts. Choose to love daily, even when emotions shift.

4. **Pray for Your Marriage Daily** – A strong marriage is built in prayer. Cover your wife in prayer. Protect your marriage spiritually.

5. **Keep Your Mind and Heart Aligned with God** – The battle for faithfulness starts in your thoughts. Stay in the Word. Seek

5. accountability. Stay connected to godly men who will challenge you to remain steadfast.

Conclusion

As men, we must recognize that commitment is not a temporary arrangement, nor is it based on conditions or convenience. Commitment, when viewed through the lens of a covenant, becomes something far deeper, far stronger, and far more enduring than any contract. It is an unshakable bond, designed by God, to stand the test of time, trials, and temptations. A contract says, "I will stay as long as you meet my expectations." But a covenant says, "I am with you through everything, whether it's easy or hard, because I promised and I chose this, not because of what you can do for me, but because of what I've committed to you before God." This covenant mindset is what keeps the fire burning—it's the fuel that burns in the heart of a One Burner Man. When challenges arise, it is this covenant that says, "I am not going anywhere." This mindset guards against complacency and motivates men to step up, pursue, protect, and cherish their wives, regardless of circumstances. Commitment in marriage, when rooted in covenant, is not only a promise to another person but also a sacred vow before God. This is why prayer is not just a ritual; it is a vital lifeline—a connection to God's strength, wisdom, and guidance as we honor the covenant we made. The commitment we make is not just to our wives but to the God who created marriage. It is God who empowers us to love sacrificially, to remain faithful, and to lead with grace and integrity. As you reflect on the idea of covenant commitment, let it sink deep into your spirit. Commitment is a choice, and it's one you make every day.

Prayer

Heavenly Father,

Thank You for the gift of marriage and the covenant I have made before You. Help me shift my mindset from a contract to a covenant, loving my wife unconditionally and leading with integrity. Give me the strength to stay committed through every season, and guide me in my words and actions. When challenges arise, may Your wisdom and grace sustain me, and may my marriage reflect Your love. Empower me to honor my vows daily, and help me to keep the fire of commitment burning bright. I trust in Your strength to lead me as a husband. **In Jesus' name, Amen.**

REFLECTION

Have I been approaching my marriage as a contract or a covenant?

_____

_____

_____

_____

_____

_____

_____

_____

_____

_____

_____

_____

_____

_____

_____

_____

_____

_____

_____

_____

_____

REFLECTION

What does my daily mindset tell me about how I view my commitment to my wife?

_____

_____

_____

_____

_____

_____

_____

_____

_____

_____

_____

_____

_____

_____

_____

_____

_____

_____

_____

_____

_____

REFLECTION

What are some practical ways I can show my wife that I am committed to her unconditionally?

_____

_____

_____

_____

_____

_____

_____

_____

_____

_____

_____

_____

_____

_____

_____

_____

_____

_____

_____

_____

_____

_____

CHAPTER THREE

Keeping the Fire Burning

The wedding day might light the match, but the marriage is what tends the flame.

Too many men believe commitment ends with saying "I do" — as if the altar is the finish line, when in truth, it's only the starting gate. The One Burner Man doesn't just burn bright for a moment; he learns to burn steady for a lifetime.

A flame left untended will die, whether it's the fire in a hearth or the fire in a heart. Marriage is much the same. It's easy to burn when love is new and the world is soft beneath your feet. But over time, the winds of life begin to blow — bills stack up like bricks, children arrive and shift the rhythm, bodies change, and the spark of excitement faces the cold realities of routine.

But here's the truth: real love isn't about keeping the fire burning by chance — it's about learning the discipline of fire-keeping.

The Gardener Of Love

A man who desires a lasting marriage must learn to become a gardener, not just a gatherer. You see, a gatherer plucks flowers when they are at their most beautiful, bright and fragrant — but he doesn't plant them, he doesn't water them, he doesn't nurture their roots. He enjoys the bloom but discards the stem when the petals fade.

A gardener, however, understands the process. He knows beauty is not something you stumble upon — it's something you cultivate. A man's love for his wife is just the same. It cannot survive on the sweetness of the wedding day or the passion of youthful desire. Love that lasts is love that is planted, tended, watered, pruned, and protected.

When a gardener wakes up each day, he does not say, "I watered the soil yesterday, so today I can forget about it." He understands that every day, the soil pulls moisture away, the sun beats down, and the winds can be harsh. So, he returns to the soil — again and again — with patience, commitment, and intention.

The same is true for a husband.

Every day life pulls at the roots of your marriage — bills, stress, unmet expectations, time pressures, misunderstandings, even your own tiredness. Love that is not nourished will wither, no matter how strong it looked in the beginning.

A One Burner Man rises every morning with the mindset:

"How can I water this garden today?"

- With kind words.
- With acts of service.
- With intentional attention.
- With prayer that covers the soil of his marriage.
- With listening ears and a humble heart.

And just like a true gardener, a man must learn the art of pruning — not everything in a marriage needs to grow. Sometimes old habits, selfish mindsets, or childish ways must be trimmed away so new growth can emerge.

A gardener doesn't abandon his garden when winter comes. He covers the soil. He guards the roots. He waits, knowing that under the surface, life is still there — even when it looks bare and cold.

In marriage, there will be seasons where passion feels dim, where laughter is rare, and connection is strained. These are the winters of love. The One Burner Man does not walk away or let the fire die. He does not panic when love looks different. Instead, he stands watch, he covers his wife in prayer, he speaks life over her even when the soil looks dry, and he waits for spring to come again. This is what it means to be the gardener of love.

Every marriage will walk through seasons:

- The spring of new love, where everything feels alive.
- The summer, when passion is easy and days are long.
- The autumn, when the newness fades and leaves begin to fall.
- The winter, when cold silence can drift between two hearts.

But a covenant man understands this: the seasons may change, but the fire must not. His love isn't seasonal, it's steady — like the sun that rises even behind the darkest clouds.

In the end, the gardener eats from the tree he once planted. The fruit of a well-tended marriage is peace, intimacy, laughter, trust, and companionship that only deepens with time. The world chases newness, but a gardener knows — the sweetest fruit comes not from something new, but from something faithfully grown.

When a man loves his wife as Christ loves the Church — not as a consumer but as a cultivator — he steps into his role as a Kingdom husband. And a Kingdom husband understands:
Love is not found. Love is grown.

In every home and in every heart, a flame needs three things to survive:

1. **Fuel** — Words and actions that affirm and uplift.
2. **Oxygen** — Space for growth, grace for mistakes, and room for God to move between you.
3. **Protection** — Guarding the flame from outside winds: temptation, neglect, and spiritual laziness.

A man who masters this will find his love doesn't flicker — it grows. He'll be known not as a man who once loved, but as a man who stayed loving.

Every fire, no matter how bright it once burned, will die without these three essentials. Marriage is no different. A One Burner Man knows that love isn't sustained by emotion alone — it is built and maintained by wisdom, intention, and the daily choice to feed the flame.

Let's break it down:

Fuel — Love Needs Substance

Fuel is what the fire consumes to stay alive. Without it, the flame will starve.

In marriage, fuel comes in the form of words, actions, and intentional investment. A man must speak life over his wife — not just once in a while, but as often as the sun rises. Words are not empty when they are spoken from a heart anchored in commitment. A compliment, an unexpected text, a note left on the bathroom mirror, or even the simple act of listening with your whole heart — these are the logs you lay on the fire.

You can't expect a fire to burn on yesterday's ashes. You can't expect your marriage to thrive on yesterday's "I love you." Love is a living thing. It hungers. It thirsts. It needs regular nourishment.

Oxygen — Space for Growth and Grace

Even the strongest fire will suffocate without oxygen. It can have the best fuel, but if it's starved of air, it will flicker out.
In marriage, oxygen represents space — the kind that lets both husband and wife breathe. It's grace. It's patience. It's the understanding that both of you are human, both will fail, both will grow. When a man strangles his marriage with control, jealousy, or selfishness, he cuts off the air supply. A wise man learns that love grows stronger not by force, but by freedom.

You have to let your wife evolve, let her passions breathe, let her voice be heard. And you must give the Holy Spirit space to move between you both. Without oxygen, even the best intentions will smother under the weight of human pride.

Protection — Guarding the Flame

The third element is protection. A fire left exposed to the wind, rain, and storms will die, no matter how much fuel and oxygen it has.

For a One Burner Man, protection means building walls around his marriage — not to trap his wife inside, but to shield the relationship from outside threats.

It's guarding your heart and mind from temptation.

It's setting healthy boundaries with other women.

It's eliminating hidden doors that lead to emotional or physical unfaithfulness.

The enemy doesn't destroy marriages overnight — it starts with small cracks: casual conversations, wandering eyes, neglected prayers, unchecked frustrations.

A wise man builds up the walls before the storm comes, not during it. He stays alert. He covers his marriage in prayer. He listens to the whispers of the Holy Spirit. And he becomes a watchman over his own heart, because he knows the fire he's been given is worth protecting.

Metaphor to Remember:

A fire is both wild and sacred. Left untended, it will die. Left unguarded, it will burn down the whole house. But when cared for with discipline, it will warm generations.

The same is true for your love.

Practical Steps: Tending the Flame Daily

1. **Cultivate Curiosity:** Never stop learning her. The woman you married will not be the same woman five, ten, or twenty years from now. Seasons will change her, and you must be willing to study her like you studied her when you were trying to win her heart. Curiosity keeps the flame alive.

2. **Build Memory Altars:** Create moments that become memorials in your marriage — not just birthdays or anniversaries, but small intentional memories: random handwritten notes, planned getaways even if it's just a park bench, simple surprises. Love needs landmarks to remind you both why you started.

3. **Speak Life Daily:** The tongue is like flint and steel — it can spark a flame or snuff it out. Speak words that fan the fire in her soul, especially when the world has tried to put it out. Your words are either water or gasoline.

4. **Stay Spiritually Fit:** A man cannot lead a wife deeper into love than he is willing to go with Christ. The fire of marriage is fed in private devotion long before it shines in public affection. A cold heart toward God often leads to a cold heart toward your wife.

5. **Master the Ministry of Listening:** Many men want to fix problems, but few learn to simply listen. Listening is an act of love. It tells your wife: "You are worth my time. Your heart matters here." A One Burner Man becomes a safe space, not just a strong presence.

6. **Set Boundaries Like Fences Around Fire:** Just as you don't leave an open flame unattended, you don't leave your marriage unguarded. Set boundaries with social media, friendships, and environments that can tempt or threaten your covenant. Fire, when contained, gives warmth. Fire, left wild, burns down homes.

7. **Celebrate Her Wins, Cover Her Losses:** When she succeeds, be her loudest cheerleader. When she struggles, be her quietest shelter. Consistent celebration and consistent compassion are fuels that no other man can supply — only you.

Conclusion

Love is not a wildfire — it's a carefully tended flame. A fire that burns wild will destroy everything in its path, but a fire that's nurtured will warm a house for generations. Passion does not die because two people fall out of love, it dies because two people stop choosing to feed it. A One Burner Man understands that keeping the fire burning is not a one-time gesture, but a daily discipline.

When the world offers convenience over covenant, thrill over trust, and comfort over commitment — you, as a kingdom husband, must choose the ancient path: faithfulness. The real measure of a man is not how fiercely he starts, but how faithfully he finishes. May your love be the kind that outlasts storms, withstands seasons, and leaves a legacy of light.

The fire is in your hands. Tend it well.

Prayer

Heavenly Father,

Teach me how to tend to the flame of love You've placed in my marriage. Remind me daily that true love isn't found in feelings alone but in faithfulness, service, and sacrifice. Help me see my wife with fresh eyes — to cherish her as the gift You have entrusted to me. Strengthen my mind, discipline my heart, and guard my steps from anything that would quench this fire. Make me a man who burns with commitment, passion, and integrity for one woman, for all the days of my life. **In Jesus' name, Amen.**

REFLECTION

Am I intentionally learning about my wife the way I did when we first met?

_____

_____

_____

_____

_____

_____

_____

_____

_____

_____

_____

_____

_____

_____

_____

_____

_____

_____

_____

_____

_____

_____

REFLECTION

What small, consistent acts am I doing to keep our love flame alive?

_____

_____

_____

_____

_____

_____

_____

_____

_____

_____

_____

_____

_____

_____

_____

_____

_____

_____

_____

_____

_____

REFLECTION

Have I allowed routine or distraction to cool the passion in my marriage?

_____

_____

_____

_____

_____

_____

_____

_____

_____

_____

_____

_____

_____

_____

_____

_____

_____

_____

_____

REFLECTION

What does "keeping the fire burning" look like in this season of our lives?

_____

_____

_____

_____

_____

_____

_____

_____

_____

_____

_____

_____

_____

_____

_____

_____

_____

_____

_____

CHAPTER FOUR
The Weight of Legacy — Building Beyond Yourself

Long after the wedding day, long after the children are grown, long after the career has quieted and your name fades from daily conversation — something still speaks. Your legacy.

A man's life was never meant to burn out for temporary pleasure or shallow ambition. It was designed by God to leave a mark that time cannot erase. Legacy is not built with hands — it's built with decisions. It's carved into history every time a man chooses principle over passion, covenant over convenience, and truth over trend.

When a man becomes a "One Burner Man," he doesn't just bless his marriage — he blesses the generations that will follow. His life becomes a blueprint for sons to imitate and for daughters to seek when choosing their own husband. He becomes a living letter written not with ink, but with character.

A Jamaican proverb says:

"The same sun that melts the butter hardens the clay."

In other words, the same environment can either make or break a man depending on the substance he's made of. Are you building a life that melts under pressure or hardens into something strong enough to last?

Your faithfulness to your wife is not just about today — it's about your name. Your commitment isn't only for your household — it's for the streets your children will walk, the rooms they'll enter, the choices they'll make. The kind of man you are sets the boundaries for the world your family will inherit.

The hard truth is this: we will all leave something behind. Whether you mean to or not, your life is writing a will — not just with your possessions, but with your patterns.

When a man lives selfishly, chasing women like wild bushfires, sowing lies, dishonor, and double-living — what outlives him is brokenness, confusion, mistrust, and pain. Generations will eat from fruit they didn't plant, but the root came from him.

But a *One Burner Man* is different. His life becomes like the strong blue mahoe tree — Jamaica's national tree — not fast to grow, but once matured, it stands tall, deep-rooted, and impossible to shake. The same storms that uproot weaker trees only prove its strength.

Every prayer you pray over your family...

Every time you hold your peace instead of starting war at home...

Every time you choose your wife over the temptation of another woman's attention...

You're adding another ring to the trunk of your legacy.

Legacy Is Built In the Quiet Moments

It's not built on stages. It's not built on how many likes you get or how much money you stack. It's built in the quiet. When no one's watching. When it's just you, your thoughts, your wife, and your God.

A real man's legacy is shaped more by what he says "no" to than what he says "yes" to.

- **No to lustful eyes.**
- **No to wandering hearts.**
- **No to easy exits.**
- **No to living for himself.**

And instead — yes to covenant.

Yes to honor.

Yes to growth, even when it's hard.

Yes to dying to self, so something greater can live.

Becoming a Living Inheritance

Ephesians 5:25

Husbands, love your wives, just as Christ loved the church and gave himself up for her

But inheritance isn't just land, or cash, or cars. The most powerful inheritance is the kind that can't be stolen or lost — a name, a reputation, a godly standard. Your legacy is the soil your children's lives will grow from.

Ask yourself: Will my name open doors or close them? Will my absence bring peace or pain? Will my children struggle to heal from me or celebrate the lessons I've left them?

This is the real weight of manhood. And this is why being a One Burner Man is about more than marriage — it's about eternity.

Legacy Is Planted, Not Purchased

You can't buy legacy in a store. You can't fake it. You can't post enough Instagram photos to secure it.

Legacy is planted like a seed — small, often unnoticed — and watered daily with integrity, sacrifice, prayer, patience, and love. The fruit shows up in the future, but the work happens today.

Imagine two men standing side by side:

One spends his life running from woman to woman, living off impulse, craving the next thrill, gathering shallow relationships like pebbles. When he dies, the world moves on like he was never there. His name fades like smoke.

The other chooses the narrow path. He loves one woman, he serves his family, he builds with wisdom, he forgives quickly, and he surrenders his ego at the feet of Christ. When his time comes, his name is a shelter. His children mention him with pride. His grandchildren carry his values even in a world gone mad.

That's the difference between living for the moment and living for eternity.

A Call to Kingdom Impact

The life of a man is more than his job title, the balance of his bank account, or the number of years he's been alive. True manhood — the kind that echoes into eternity — leaves an impact. Not just an impression, not just a moment of applause, but a deep, lasting mark on this earth and in heaven.

A Kingdom man isn't built for comfort, convenience, or applause. He's built for impact.

The world teaches men to chase influence. Influence fades. Kingdom impact outlives you.

A man of God doesn't just want to "make it." He wants to make a difference.

Most men grow up fighting to survive — for respect, for money, for a place at the table. But God never designed His sons to settle for survival. The call to be a Kingdom man is a call to rise from survival to significance.

When a man surrenders his life to Christ, he trades shallow success for eternal significance. His words begin to carry weight. His love is no longer cheap. His faithfulness becomes his testimony. His marriage becomes a ministry. His household becomes a training ground for future world-changers.

You see, when God calls a man, He never calls him alone. The call is not just for your benefit. It's for the generations behind you, the community around you, and the legacy that will outlive you.

A Kingdom man lives for more than his own name.

He lives for the name above all names — Jesus.

When you submit your desires, your pride, your ambitions to God, you make room for divine impact. Your life becomes a seed planted in the soil of eternity, destined to bear fruit long after your time on this earth is done.

Imagine a man standing by the sea, holding a lantern in a raging storm. His job is simple — keep the light burning so ships can find their way safely home. He doesn't chase after the ships, and he doesn't command the sea. He simply holds his ground and keeps the flame alive.

A Kingdom man is like that lighthouse keeper.

He stands on the solid rock of Christ.

He holds the light of truth and love steady.

And even when the waves crash against his life, his marriage, and his family, he refuses to let the light go out.

Because somewhere out there, another soul is navigating the dark — and your faithfulness could lead them home.

Practical Steps to Build a Legacy as a One Burner Man

1. **Lead with Integrity** - Even in Private - Legacy isn't built in front of an audience — it's built in the quiet, unseen

1. decisions. Choose honesty when nobody's watching. Integrity is the foundation your family will stand on.

2. **Speak Life Daily** - Your words shape the world of your wife and your children. Use your voice to encourage, affirm, and bless. Let them hear you speak vision, faith, and hope even on hard days.

3. **Stay Teachable, Stay Humble** - A legacy man never stops learning. Whether through Scripture, mentors, or life experience, stay humble enough to grow. Your example will teach your family that strength and humility walk hand in hand.

4. **Prioritize Prayer Over Pressure** - When life becomes overwhelming, don't react — retreat into prayer. A man of prayer builds a home rooted in peace, even when storms surround it.

5. **Invest Time, Not Just Money** - Wealth can run out, but memories and moments last a lifetime. Spend intentional time with your wife, children, and family — be present, be fully there.

6. **Decide Once, Every Day** - Legacy isn't built on a single grand moment — it's shaped by daily decisions. Every morning, decide again: "I will love, I will lead, I will be faithful."

Conclusion

A man's true success is measured not by the size of his house, the balance of his bank account, or the power of his position — but by the strength of his legacy. A One Burner Man lives for more than just his own pleasure; he lives for the glory of God, the security of his family, and the blessing of future generations. When you choose covenant over convenience, when you choose faithfulness over fleeting passion, you write a story that will echo long after your time on earth is done.

Your name can be the greatest inheritance your family ever receives.

Make sure it's one worth carrying.

Prayer

Heavenly Father,

Teach me to be a man who builds beyond himself. Let my life reflect Your love, Your faithfulness, and Your wisdom. Help me to walk with integrity in both the quiet places and the crowded rooms. Let my marriage be a testimony of covenant love, and may my children and those who follow behind me find strength in the foundation I lay today. Strip away selfishness and short-sightedness, and replace it with purpose, vision, and grace. Help me to honor the legacy You've given me and to leave one that brings You glory.

In Jesus' name, Amen.

REFLECTION

Am I living today with future generations in mind, or only for my own comfort and convenience?

_____

_____

_____

_____

_____

_____

_____

_____

_____

_____

_____

_____

_____

_____

_____

_____

_____

_____

_____

_____

_____

_____

REFLECTION

What kind of man do I want my children or those
watching me to remember?

_____

_____

_____

_____

_____

_____

_____

_____

_____

_____

_____

_____

_____

_____

_____

_____

_____

_____

_____

_____

_____

_____

REFLECTION

How am I investing in the spiritual growth of my
household beyond providing financially?

_____

_____

_____

_____

_____

_____

_____

_____

_____

_____

_____

_____

_____

_____

_____

_____

_____

_____

_____

_____

REFLECTION

In what areas of my life do I need to start choosing integrity over convenience?

_____

_____

_____

_____

_____

_____

_____

_____

_____

_____

_____

_____

_____

_____

_____

_____

_____

_____

_____

_____

REFLECTION

What old habits or mindsets do I need to break so that I don't pass them on to the next generation?

_____

_____

_____

_____

_____

_____

_____

_____

_____

_____

_____

_____

_____

_____

_____

_____

_____

_____

_____

_____

_____

CHAPTER FIVE

Safe to Be Soft — Emotional Safety and Vulnerability in a Man's Marriage

In many cultures — especially in Caribbean, African, and even traditional Christian homes — men are taught to be strong. Stoic. Providers. Protectors. The rocks of the family.

But what happens when the rock starts to crack?

What happens when the man feels things he can't name? When he's drowning in pressure but doesn't know how to say, "I'm not okay"? When he doesn't even know how to feel, let alone express it?

This chapter is a call to break the silence around emotional vulnerability. It's a call to teach men that being a "One Burner Man" doesn't just mean sexual faithfulness — it means emotional faithfulness too. It means creating a marriage where you're not just safe to protect — you're safe to be soft.

From a young age, many men were handed invisible bricks — and told, "Build."

Each brick carried a message:

"Man up."

"Stop crying before I give you something to cry about."

"Real men don't need to talk."

"Strength is silence."

"Nobody cares about your feelings."

So brick by brick, without even realizing it, he built.

Not a house. Not a legacy.

But a fortress — around his emotions, his fears, and his truth.

At first, that wall felt like safety.

It kept out ridicule. It protected him from judgment.

It helped him survive environments where softness was a liability.

But over time, the same wall that shielded him also shut people out.

His wife tries to reach for him — but her words bounce off stone.

His children sense a distance they can't explain.

He's in the room — but emotionally, he's locked behind years of silence.

He loves them.

Deeply. Fiercely.

But love that is never expressed begins to feel like absence.

And what once looked like strength now just feels like emotional isolation.

The world often mistakes emotionally distant men for unfeeling ones.

But in truth, most of them are not cold — they're conditioned. Conditioned to survive instead of connect.

To protect instead of process.

To perform instead of feel.

He doesn't know how to say, "I'm not okay."

He was taught that vulnerability is exposure — and exposure is weakness.

So he carries his battles like a soldier in silence, wearing smiles as armor.

And his wife — the woman he vowed to cleave to, body and soul — starts to feel like she's married to a ghost.

Not because he's left...but because his emotional presence never fully arrived.

What Emotional Absence Looks Like

It doesn't always scream. Sometimes it just fades:

- He answers with one-word responses.
- He's quick to fix but slow to listen.
- He works more, talks less.
- He avoids deep conversations.
- He only shows joy or anger — but nothing in between.

The marriage becomes functional. Routine. Surface-level.

And though the house is still standing, the soul of the home begins to dry up.

It's not infidelity that broke them.

It's not abuse.

It's the **quiet pain of disconnection.**

That emotional wall? It doesn't just affect the marriage.

It spills into fatherhood.

Into friendships.

Even into his walk with God. Because a man who doesn't know how to open up emotionally to his wife, often struggles to open up spiritually to his Father.

He avoids stillness.

He numbs instead of feeling.

He performs for God but doesn't pour out to Him.

That wall around his heart becomes a prison.

And the key isn't found in performing harder — but in healing deeper.

What Emotional Safety Looks Like

Emotional safety in marriage is when a man can:

- Admit when he's afraid, without being judged.
- Cry in front of his wife and still feel respected.
- Say "I don't know what to do," and not lose his leadership.
- Share what's really going on inside — not just what sounds spiritual or strong.

It's when the wife doesn't just see the man's strength — she sees his heart.

And he knows: "I don't have to hide here. I'm safe."

How to Become Emotionally Safe

1. Learn the Language of Emotion

Many men were never taught to name what they feel.

It's like standing in a fire and only knowing how to say, "It's hot."

But emotional safety starts when a man learns how to speak the inner language of his own soul.

"I'm fine" is not a feeling — it's a cover.

And what's buried alive in silence will eventually rise in behavior.

When a man says:

"I feel rejected."

"I feel disrespected."

"I feel overlooked."

"I feel anxious about providing."

he's not being weak — he's being honest. And where there is truth, there is room for healing.

Learning this language is like unlocking a prison cell — one word at a time. Start simple. Use emotional check-ins. Even Jesus wept. Even David cried out in the Psalms. Real men feel deeply. Kingdom men **express intentionally.**

2. Make Time to Slow Down

You can't hear your heart if you're always sprinting.

Busyness is one of the most spiritual ways the enemy dulls emotional awareness.

Because when life gets loud, the soul goes quiet. Slowing down isn't laziness — it's stewardship of the heart. It's how a man pauses long enough to say:

"What am I carrying today?"

"Why am I irritated?"

Build sacred pauses into your routine — a walk without a phone, a moment after work where you sit in silence, a Sabbath rest where you don't just recover physically, but emotionally.

Slowing down gives your soul room to speak, and your spirit space to listen.

3. Ask for Help Without Shame

Most men would rather bleed in silence than admit they're wounded.

But the kingdom man understands: wisdom is not knowing everything — it's knowing when to ask.

Even Jesus had Simon help carry His cross.

So why do men feel like they must carry theirs alone?

Asking for help is not failure. It's faith.

- Faith that someone can walk with you through this.
- Faith that vulnerability will not destroy your dignity.
- Faith that healing is possible — but not always solo.

Find a counselor. Open up to a trusted mentor. Talk to a pastor who's walked the road.

Let another man speak life into the places you've buried.

You're not meant to fix what you can't even see.

You need mirrors, not just muscles.

4. Invite Your Wife In

She doesn't just want your presence. She wants your person.

Not the provider, not the planner, not just the protector.

She wants the real you — fears, failures, and all.

That's what covenant is.

Naked and unashamed. Emotionally exposed and still fully embraced.

Let her in. Let her hold the parts of you you were taught to hide. Because love is not real until it meets the parts of us we're most tempted to withhold.

Say to her,

"I don't have all the answers right now."

"I'm scared of failing you."

"I feel lost sometimes."

And watch how trust deepens when performance dies. This isn't about dumping your pain on her — it's about inviting her into your process.

You were never meant to go through manhood like a lone soldier.

Let love in. Let her in.

What Grows From Vulnerability

When a man chooses to become emotionally safe, something powerful begins to shift — not just in him, but around him. He no longer walks through life armored up, reacting to every perceived threat or challenge with defensiveness, aggression, or silence.

Instead, he begins to relate — soul to soul, not role to role.

His posture softens, but his presence strengthens.

Why?

Because true vulnerability doesn't strip a man of his masculinity — it grounds it in purpose.

When a man is emotionally unsafe, his marriage becomes a battlefield — small triggers turn into big wars.

But when he learns to pause, to reflect, and to express what's going on inside him, he stops reacting from past wounds and starts relating from present wholeness.

- Instead of lashing out in frustration, he can say, "I'm feeling overwhelmed right now."
- Instead of shutting down, he can say, "I'm not sure how to talk about this, but I want to try."

These small moments of vulnerability plant seeds of peace.

And peace is not passive — it's powerful.

When a man becomes emotionally safe, his wife doesn't feel like she has to "guess" how he's doing.

She no longer walks on eggshells, wondering if he's angry, distant, or just tired.

Instead, she feels invited into his heart, not just his routine. She becomes more than just the one he protects — she becomes the one he trusts.

And for a woman, that emotional access is sacred.

It's intimacy beyond the bedroom.

It's safety beyond provision.

It's the quiet knowing:

"I'm not just loved for what I do — I'm loved for who I am."

Children Who Witness Emotional Wisdom

Vulnerability doesn't just heal a marriage — it rewrites the legacy. A father who speaks the language of emotion teaches his children that manhood is not measured by how much you hide, but how well you love.

He becomes a safe place for his daughter to trust and his son to emulate.

His presence isn't just in discipline, but in understanding.

When your children see you express, not suppress — when they hear, "Daddy's sad today, but it's okay to feel sad," they learn that emotions are not enemies. They're messengers.

And fathers who are emotionally available raise emotionally whole children.

Many men build houses full of rules. Few build homes full of refuge.

Structure matters. Discipline matters. Leadership matters.

But when there is no emotional warmth — the structure feels like a cage, not a covering.

A home becomes holy when it carries:

- A father who embraces tears and questions.
- A man who leads not just with instructions — but with intentional connection.

Vulnerability turns a cold house into a warm sanctuary.

It creates a culture where love doesn't have to be earned — it's experienced daily.

Vulnerability doesn't erase your strength — it redeems it.

It's not weakness to say, "I need prayer."

It's not weakness to say, "I'm hurting."

That's not a man falling apart.

That's a man becoming **whole.**

Your softness — your willingness to feel, to express, to invite others into your inner world — is not your undoing.

It's your **anointing.**

It is the oil that transforms leadership from pressure into presence.

It is the grace that takes your marriage from a contract to a covenant.

It is the wisdom that turns ordinary love into **holy ground.**

A man who is only needed becomes exhausted.

But a man who is also known becomes fulfilled.

Your wife doesn't just want a provider — she wants a partner.

Someone who is in it with her.

Heart, mind, and soul.

When she no longer feels like she has to earn your attention, decode your silence, or beg for your emotion —she begins to flourish.

And when your marriage moves from a place of survival to mutual surrender, you begin to taste the delight God designed for covenant love.

Conclusion

Vulnerability is not a side-note in the life of a kingdom man — it is a central, holy practice.

It is not optional for those who want lasting love.

It is the bridge that turns connection into communion, distance into intimacy, and survival into sacred union.

When a man chooses to drop the mask, he doesn't lose his authority — he deepens it.

When he opens the door to his inner world, he gives his wife and children permission to enter — and that is where true closeness begins.

You were not created to be a fortress with locked doors.

You were created to be a well — deep, open, and life-giving.

Your emotional depth is not your downfall.

It's your design.

And when you surrender that design to God, you don't just

become a good husband —

you become a kingdom man.

Prayer

Father,

Thank You for showing me that strength and softness can live together. I lay down the lies that told me emotions are weakness and vulnerability is dangerous. I ask You to rewire my heart and teach me the language of truth. Help me to become a safe place — not only for my wife, but for my children, and for myself. Strip away the emotional walls I've built from pain, pride, or fear. Make me the kind of man who leads with tenderness, listens with intention, and loves without hiding. Let the softness of my spirit be the sign of Your strength within me.

In Jesus' name, Amen.

REFLECTION

Where in my life have I confused silence with strength?

_____

_____

_____

_____

_____

_____

_____

_____

_____

_____

_____

_____

_____

_____

_____

_____

_____

_____

_____

_____

REFLECTION

How did my upbringing shape the way I view emotions
and vulnerability?

_____

_____

_____

_____

_____

_____

_____

_____

_____

_____

_____

_____

_____

_____

_____

_____

_____

_____

_____

_____

REFLECTION

Have I ever invited my wife into my internal world — or
just my physical one?

_____

_____

_____

_____

_____

_____

_____

_____

_____

_____

_____

_____

_____

_____

_____

_____

_____

_____

_____

REFLECTION

How does vulnerability feel threatening to me — and why?

_____

_____

_____

_____

_____

_____

_____

_____

_____

_____

_____

_____

_____

_____

_____

_____

_____

_____

_____

_____

REFLECTION

When was the last time I slowed down long enough to really check in with myself?

_____

_____

_____

_____

_____

_____

_____

_____

_____

_____

_____

_____

_____

_____

_____

_____

_____

The One Burner Man

There's a man the world doesn't talk about much anymore.

He's not flashy.

He's not chasing applause.

He doesn't need twenty women to feel like a man.

He just needs one.

He's the man who burns for one woman — who turns down the noise, silences the culture, and plants himself in covenant.

He's the one burner man.

And he's not extinct.

He's just been buried under broken examples, loud distractions, and unhealed wounds.

But now — you've heard the call.

This book has not been about perfection.

It's been about intention.

It's not a list of rules, but a roadmap to becoming — not just a husband, but a kingdom husband.

Becoming a one burner man isn't a one-time decision.

It's a daily surrender.

It's waking up every morning and saying:

- "I choose her again."

- "I choose love again."
- "I choose to lead with grace, not ego."
- "I choose to be known, not just respected."

It means guarding your flame — not just from other women, but from pride, distraction, bitterness, and passivity.

Because fires don't die in a day.

They die when they're neglected.

So keep tending to your fire.

Keep stoking it with prayer, humility, honesty, and presence.

When one man burns for one woman, he shifts the culture.

He teaches his sons that loyalty is not boring — it's powerful.

He shows his daughters what it means to be chosen, not used.

He becomes a pillar in his home, his church, and his community — not because he's loud, but because he's anchored.

The one burner man is a man who builds legacy.

And if you're reading this — then you are being called into that legacy now.

You may stumble.

You may feel lost some days.

You may feel like your past disqualifies you. But hear this:

God is not looking for the perfect man —

He's looking for the willing one.

He'll take your ashes and give you beauty.

He'll take your broken pieces and make you whole.

He'll take your surrendered heart and turn it into a fire that never goes out.

So choose the path of one woman.

Choose the way of the cross.

Choose to become a man who doesn't just say "I love you" —
but lives it every day.

You are not just a man.

You are a kingdom man.

A one burner man.

And the world needs you.

A Prayer of Becoming

Father,

Thank You for calling me higher. Thank You for showing me that I don't need the world's version of manhood — I need Yours. I lay down every false identity, every broken pattern, and every fear I've carried. I don't want to live with divided fire. I want to burn for one woman. I want to be faithful — not just in action, but in thought, in heart, and in spirit. Teach me how to lead with love. Teach me how to serve with strength. Teach me how to be tender without fear, and present without shame. Let me be a safe place for my wife, a steady presence for my children, and a light in a world that's lost the meaning of commitment. I can't do this in my own power. But by Your Spirit — I will become a one burner man.

Not for applause.

Not for perfection.

But because You have called me to this kind of love.

A covenant kind of love.

A kingdom kind of love.

Let my life reflect that.

In Jesus' name, Amen.

www.ingramcontent.com/pod-product-compliance
Lightning Source LLC
Chambersburg PA
CBHW032027090426
42741CB00006B/764